The Complete Cynic's Calendar Of Revised Wisdom: By Oliver Herford, Ethel Watts Mumford, Addison Mizner...

Oliver Herford, Ethel Watts Mumford Grant, Addison Mizner

"Now the well of truth
'Tis an ink well."

—Sayings of Towanda.

The Complete
Cynic's Calendar
of Revised Wisdom
1906

by

Ethel Watts Mumford
Oliver Herford
Addison Mizner

Paul Elder and Company
Publishers, San Francisco

Verbum Sap

The Tomoyé Press
San Francisco

DEDICATION

TO THE WORLD AT LARGE

This Little Book of Wisdom Great
It pleases us to dedicate
To that Rampageous Reprobate —
    The World at Large.
Yet as we mark his Stony Phiz
And see him whoop and whirl and whiz,
We can but cry — O Lord, why *is*
    The World at Large!

OLIVER HERFORD.

Memoranda

God gives us our
relatives — thank God
we can choose
our friends.

January

Tell the truth and
shame the — family.

Monday	1
Tuesday	2
Wednesday	3
Thursday	4
Friday	5
Saturday	6

Memoranda

Misery loves company,
but company
does not reciprocate.

Jan.

There's none so blind
as those who
won't fee.

Sunday 7

Monday 8

Tuesday 9

Wednesday 10

Thursday 11

Friday 12

Saturday 13

Memoranda

Look before you
sleep.

Jan.

Knowledge is power—
if you know it
about the right person.

Memoranda

If the wolf be at the
door, open it and
eat him.

January

A little spark may
smirk unseen.

Sunday 21

Monday 22

Tuesday 23

Wednesday 24

Thursday 25

Friday **26**

Saturday **27**

Memoranda

Many are called but
few get up.

January

The wages of Gin
is Debt.

Sunday 28
Monday 29
Tuesday 30
Wednesday 31

Feb.

Some are born widows,
some achieve widow-
hood, whilst others have
widows thrust upon
them.

Thursday   1

Friday   2

Saturday   3

Memoranda

Those that came to
cough remained
to spray.

Feb.

Actresses will happen
in the best
regulated families.

Sunday 4

Monday 5

Tuesday 6

Wednesday 7

Thursday 8

Friday 9

Saturday 10

Memoranda

"The grinders may
cease"—but the
grind goes on forever.

February

Too many hooks
spoil the cloth.

Sunday 11

Monday 12

Tuesday 13

Wednesday 14

Thursday 15

Friday 16

Saturday 17

 Memoranda

It's a strong stomach
that has no
turning.

You may lead an Ass to Knowledge—
but you cannot make him Think.

Memoranda

Friendship is more
to be valued than love,
for love is a thing a man
can buy and a woman
can get for nothing.

February

One good turn
deserves applause.

Sunday	18
Monday	19
Tuesday	20
Wednesday	21
Thursday	22
Friday	23
Saturday	24
Sunday	25
Monday	26
Tuesday	27
Wednesday	28

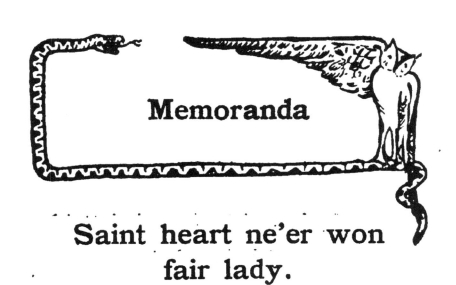

Memoranda

Saint heart ne'er won
fair lady.

Mar.

He who owes nothing
fears nothing.

Sunday 4

Monday 5

Tuesday 6

Wednesday 7

Thursday 8

Friday 9

Saturday 10

Memoranda

Silence gives contempt.

March

You will never miss
water while the
champagne runs dry.

Sunday 11

Monday 12

Tuesday 13

Wednesday 14

Thursday 15

Friday 16

Saturday 17

Memoranda

People who love
in glass houses should
pull down the blinds.

 AND

I'll make insurance doubly sure and
take a brand of fate.

Memoranda

Honor is
without profit—in most
countries.

March

Money makes the
Mayor go.

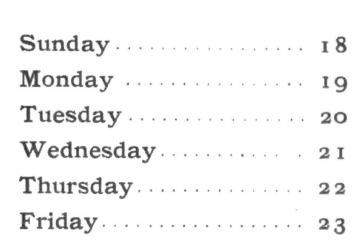

Sunday 18

Monday 19

Tuesday 20

Wednesday 21

Thursday 22

Friday 23

Saturday 24

Memoranda

A church fair exchange
is robbery.

Mar.

There's a Pen for the wise, but alas! no Pound for the foolish.

Sunday 25

Monday 26

Tuesday 27

Wednesday 28

Thursday 29

Friday 30

Saturday 31

Memoranda

Fools rush in
and win—where angels
fear to tread.

April

Imagination makes cowards of us all.

Sunday 1

Monday 2

Tuesday 3

Wednesday 4

Thursday 5

Friday 6

Saturday 7

The quill is as mighty
off the wing.

April

Wild oats make a bad
autumn crop.

Sunday 8

Monday 9

Tuesday 10

Wednesday 11

Thursday 12

Friday 13

Saturday 14

Memoranda

A rich man
can get the eye of
the beadle.

April

The number of a
man's widows will
be in proportion to
the size of his estate.

Sunday 15
Monday 16
Tuesday 17
Wednesday 18
Thursday 19
Friday 20
Saturday 21

The First Lesson.

He that is down need
not fear plucking.

Sunday 22
Monday 23
Tuesday 24
Wednesday 25
Thursday 26
Friday 27
Saturday 28
Sunday 29
Monday 30

Memoranda

Consistency, thou
art a mule!

Bubble, bubble, toil and trouble.

—Shakespeare.

Memoranda

Economy is the thief
of time.

May

Let him that standeth
pat take heed lest
they call.

Tuesday   1

Wednesday   2

Thursday   3

Friday   4

Saturday   5

A bird on a
bonnet is worth ten
on a plate.

May

Don't take the Will
for the Deed —
get the Deed.

Sunday 6

Monday 7

Tuesday 8

Wednesday 9

Thursday 10

Friday 11

Saturday 12

Memoranda

Displays are dan-
gerous.

May

The doors of
Opportunity are marked
"Push" and "Pull."

Sunday 13
Monday 14
Tuesday 15
Wednesday 16
Thursday 17
Friday 18
Saturday 19

Memoranda

Let him now speak
or hereafter hold his
piece of information
for a good price.

May

Nothing succeeds
like — failure.

Sunday 20

Monday 21

Tuesday 22

Wednesday 23

Thursday 24

Friday 25

Saturday 26

Memoranda

The poor ye have with
ye always—but are
not invited.

May

Charity is the
sterilized milk
of human kindness.

Sunday 27

Monday 28

Tuesday 29

Wednesday 30

Thursday 31

What is home without another?

June

The greatest
possession is
Self-possession.

Friday	1
Saturday	2
Sunday	3
Monday	4
Tuesday	5
Wednesday	6
Thursday	7
Friday	8
Saturday	9

Memoranda

One touch of nature
makes the whole
world squirm.

 AND

The First Monday.

Memoranda

Eat your steak or
you'll have stew.

June

Pleasant company
always accepted.

Memoranda

Stays make waist.

June

The gossip is not
always of the swift,
nor the tattle
of the wrong.

As you sew so must
you rip.

June

Advice to Parents—
"Cast not your girls
before swains."

Sunday................ 24

Monday 25

Tuesday 26

Wednesday........... 27

Thursday............. 28

Friday................ 29

Saturday 30

Memoranda

A lie in time saves nine.

July

Only the young
die good.

Sunday 1

Monday 2

Tuesday 3

Wednesday 4

Thursday 5

Friday 6

Saturday **7**

Memoranda

A thing of duty is
an — noy forever.

July

THE DOCTOR'S MOTTO—

A fee in the hand is worth two on the book.

Sunday	8
Monday	9
Tuesday	10
Wednesday	11
Thursday	12
Friday	13
Saturday	14

Memoranda

A fool and his honey
are soon mated.

 AND

July

It's better to be a
live "Lobster" than a
dead "Social Lion."

Sunday 15

Monday 16

Tuesday 17

Wednesday 18

Thursday 19

Friday 20

Saturday 21

He laughs best whose
laugh lasts.

The wisest reflections are
but Vanity.

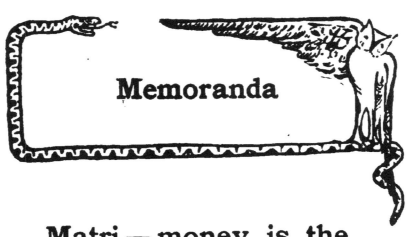

Memoranda

Matri — money is the
root of all evil.

July

Give an inch
and take an ell.

Sunday 22
Monday 23
Tuesday 24
Wednesday 25
Thursday 26
Friday 27
Saturday 28
Sunday 29
Monday 30
Tuesday 31

Memoranda

Necessity is the mother
of contention.

August

What can't be cured
must be insured.

Wednesday 1

Thursday 2

Friday 3

Saturday 4

Memoranda

Sweet are the uses
of diversity.

August

The more taste,
the less creed.

Memoranda

A word to the wise
is resented.

Aug.

There is no time
like the pleasant.

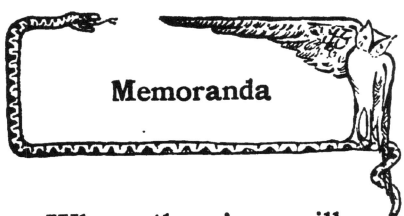

Memoranda

Where there's a will
there's a law suit.

Aug.

The danger lies not
in the big ears
of little pitchers, but
in the large mouths.

Sunday 19

Monday 20

Tuesday 21

Wednesday 22

Thursday 23

Friday 24

Saturday 25

Memoranda

Think of your ancestors
and your posterity
and you will never
marry.

August

He jests at scores
who never
played at Bridge.

Sunday 26

Monday 27

Tuesday 28

Wednesday 29

Thursday 30

Friday 31

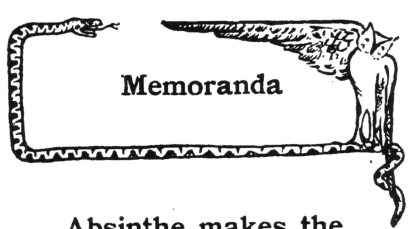

Memoranda

Absinthe makes the
heart grow fonder.

"With all thy faults I love
thee — still."

Hell is paved with big
pretensions.

September

Women change their
minds a dozen times
a day — that's why
they are so
clean-minded.

Saturday 1
Sunday 2
Monday 3
Tuesday 4
Wednesday 5
Thursday 6
Friday 7
Saturday 8

Memoranda

"Mercy and truth are
met together, righteous-
ness and peace have
kissed each other."
Look out!!!!

Sept.

Kind hearts are more
than coronets — few
girls can afford to
have either.

Sunday 9

Monday 10

Tuesday 11

Wednesday 12

Thursday 13

Friday 14

Saturday 15

Pride will have a
Fall bonnet.

Sept.

He who fights and
runs away
Will live to write
about the fray.

Sunday 16

Monday 17

Tuesday **18**

Wednesday **19**

Thursday **20**

Friday **21**

Saturday **22**

When folly is bliss 'tis ignorance
to be otherwise.

September

A gentle lie
turneth away inquiry.

Sunday 23
Monday 24
Tuesday 25
Wednesday 26
Thursday 27
Friday 28
Saturday **29**
Sunday **30**

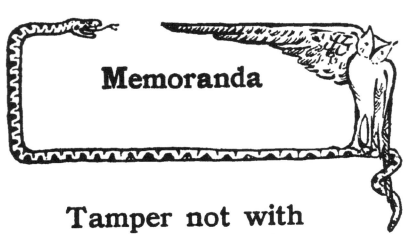

Memoranda

Tamper not with
fledged fools.

October

Never too old
to yearn.

Monday	1
Tuesday	2
Wednesday	3
Thursday	4
Friday	5
Saturday	6

Memoranda

Young widows in ash-
cloth and sashes.

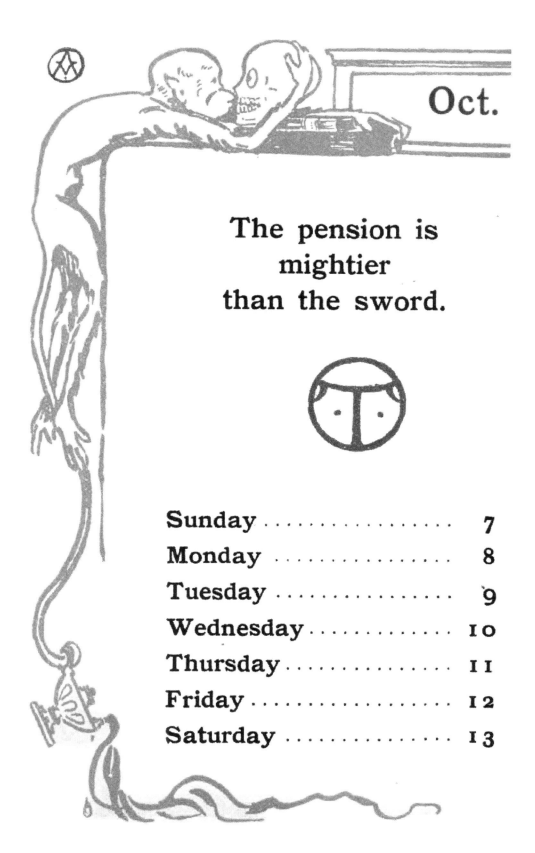

The pension is
mightier
than the sword.

Sunday   7

Monday   8

Tuesday   9

Wednesday 10

Thursday 11

Friday 12

Saturday 13

Memoranda

Pride goeth before and
the bill cometh after.

Dead men tell no tales —?—?—!

Memoranda

Tomorrow would be
sweet if we could
kill yesterday.

Oct.

A fool's paradise
is nevertheless
a paradise.

Sunday................ 14

Monday 15

Tuesday.............. 16

Wednesday........... 17

Thursday............ 18

Friday 19

Saturday 20

Memoranda

There is no soak with-
out some fire water.

October

Let Well enough alone
—there's brandy
and soda.

Sunday 21
Monday 22
Tuesday 23
Wednesday 24
Thursday 25
Friday 26
Saturday 27
Sunday 28
Monday 29
Tuesday **30**
Wednesday **31**

Memoranda

As thou hast
made thy bed, why lie
about it?

November

A fellow failing
makes us
wondrous unkind.

Thursday 1
Friday 2
Saturday 3
Sunday 4
Monday 5
Tuesday 6
Wednesday 7
Thursday 8
Friday 9
Saturday 10

Many hands want light work.

Nov.

Society covers a
multitude of sins.

Memoranda

In one's old coterie
may one sport the old
pantry and vestry?

Nov.

All is not bold
that titters.

Memoranda

It is better to make
friends fast than to
make fast friends.

November

The ways of the
transgressor
are smooth.

Sunday 25
Monday 26
Tuesday 27
Wednesday 28
Thursday 29
Friday **30**

Memoranda

Fain would I write yet
fear to pall.

Many bands make tight work.

Memoranda

A little widow is a
dangerous thing.

December

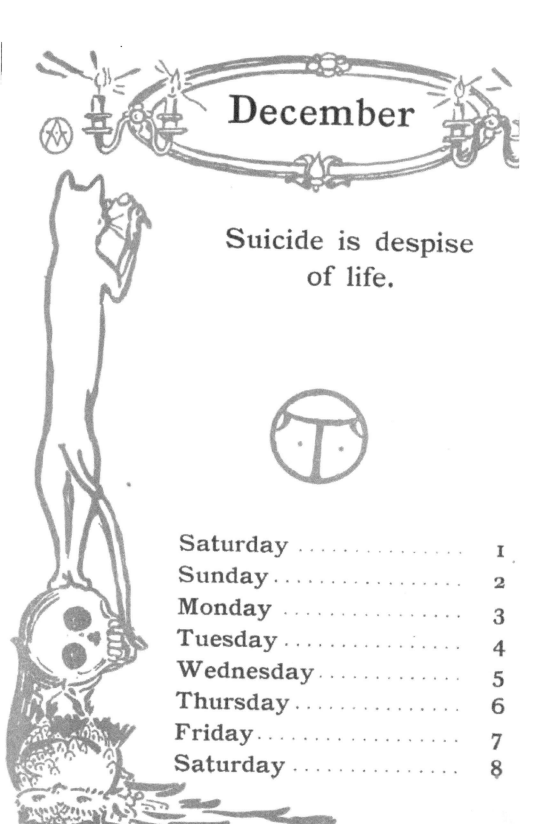

Suicide is despise
of life.

Saturday 1
Sunday 2
Monday 3
Tuesday 4
Wednesday 5
Thursday 6
Friday 7
Saturday 8

Memoranda

There's many a sip
'twixt the cup and the
lip.

THE STEAMER'S MOTTO —

You can't eat your cake and have it too.

Sunday 9

Monday 10

Tuesday 11

Wednesday 12

Thursday 13

Friday 14

Saturday 15

A friend in deeds
is a friend indeed.

Dec.

The more waist
the less speed.

Memoranda

All that a man
knoweth will he tell
to his wife.

AND

December

The self-made man
is often proud
of a poor job.

Memoranda

He that is surety
for a stranger shall be
wiser the next time.

your mouth and open your eyes—
you'll need nothing to make you wise.

Next!

Lightning Source UK Ltd.
Milton Keynes UK
UKHW030312230620
365391UK00013BA/3101